Animal Spikes and Spines

Claws

Rebecca Rissman

Heinemann Library
Chicago, Illinois

www.heinemannraintree.com
Visit our website to find out more information about Heinemann-Raintree books.

To order:
☎ Phone 888-454-2279
📠 Visit www.heinemannraintree.com to browse our catalog and order online.

Edited by Rebecca Rissman, Dan Nunn
  and Sian Smith
Designed by Joanna Hinton-Malivoire
Picture research by Tracy Cummins
Production by Victoria Fitzgerald
Originated by Capstone Global Library Ltd
Printed and bound in China by Leo Paper Products Ltd

15 14 13 12 11
10 9 8 7 6 5 4 3 2 1

Library of Congress Cataloging-in-Publication Data
Rissman, Rebecca.
  Claws / Rebecca Rissman.
    p. cm.—(Animal spikes and spines)
  Includes bibliographical references and index.
  ISBN 978-1-4329-5039-2 (hc)—ISBN 978-1-4329-5046-0 (pb)
  1. Claws—Juvenile literature. I. Title.
  QL942.R574 2012
  591.47—dc22   2010044791

Acknowledgments
Ardea p **11** (Francois Gohier); Getty Images pp **15** & **16** (both Tom Vezo); istockphoto pp **7** (© Brent Melton), **20** (© Jason Lugo), **21** (© Bob Ingelhart); National Geographic Stock pp **12** (Norbert Wu/Minden Pictures); Photolibrary pp **6** (Pierre Huguet), **9** & **10** (both Juniors Bildarchiv); Shutterstock pp **4** (© Godrick), **5** (© 9744444159), **8** (© Mogens Trolle), **17**, **18** & **22** (all © Pshenichka), **23a** (© Mogens Trolle); Visuals Unlimited, Inc. pp **13**, **14** & **23b** (all David Wrobel).

Cover photograph of a crab with its pincers raised on a beach, reproduced with permission of Getty Images (Bob Elsdale). Back cover photograph of a cat reproduced with permission of Shutterstock (© 9744444159).

We would like to thank Michael Bright, Nancy Harris, Dee Reid, and Diana Bentley for their assistance in the preparation of this book.

Every effort has been made to contact copyright holders of material reproduced in this book. Any omissions will be rectified in subsequent printings if notice is given to the publisher.

Contents

Animal Body Parts

Animals have different body parts.

claws

Some animals have claws.

What Are Claws?

paw

Claws are hard, sharp nails.

Claws grow from animals' paws.

Claws help animals in many ways.

Different Claws

Claws can look very different.

Some claws are very sharp.
What animal is this?

This animal is a tiger. It uses its claws
to help it hunt.

Some claws are big and long.
What animal is this?

This animal is a sloth. It uses its claws to help it climb trees.

pincers

Some claws are called pincers.

What animal is this?

This animal is a lobster. It uses its claws to catch food.

Some claws are short and curved.
What animal is this?

This animal is a caracara. It uses its claws to hold on to branches.

Some claws are very small.
What animal is this?

This animal is a rat. It uses its claws to
dig and to hold food.

Your Body

Do you have claws?

No! Humans do not have claws.

Humans have fingernails and toenails.

Can You Remember?

Which animal uses its claws to dig and hold food?

Picture glossary

claws long, hard, pointed nails on an animal's paws. A lobster or a crab's pincers are also called claws.

pincers claws of a crab or a lobster that come together to hold things tightly

Index

Notes for Parents and Teachers

Before reading

Show the children the front cover of the book. Guide them in a discussion about what they think the book will be about. Can they think of ways that animals use their claws? List their ideas on paper. Discuss how claws are body parts and the way in which animals can use their claws to do different things.

After reading

- Reference the list that you created before you read the book. Ask children if their predictions about claws were true.

- Ask the children to draw a picture of their favorite animal that they read about in the book. Children can go on to write a sentence about how that animal uses its claws or to act this out for the class.

24